TWENTY FIRST CENTURY

COTSWOLDS

The transformation of historic and character Cotswold buildings
for life in the 21st century

PIPPA PATON

Painswick Valley, Cotswolds

For Max, Scarlett and my late mother who still inspires me in everything that I do

And for Scott who brings my ideas to life

CONTENTS

Snowshill, Cotswolds

FOREWORD

b y

MARK HEDGES

The Editor-in-Chief of Country Life moved at the age of eight from Berkshire to a manor house just outside Chipping Norton in the Cotswolds. He explored the area on his pony with his Labrador trotting along beside him and quickly fell in love with the gently rolling hills and the beautiful houses built of the famous golden limestone.

Is anywhere on earth as clearly defined by its local stone as the Cotswolds? In the late evening sun, the villages look part of a fairy story with their golden, glowing masonry built out of butter and marmalade. The warm, mellow limestone seems, as JB Priestley wrote, 'to hold the sunlight of centuries'. It is the stone, above all, that gives the area harmony. It is England at its best.

This soft stone, an oolitic limestone, laid down during the Jurassic period, 142 million to 205 million years ago, is a stonemason's dream, but it was Cotswold sheep, vast flocks of them dotted across the landscape that, for centuries, provided the wealth to dig the quarries and build the Perpendicular churches, Tudor manor houses, market squares and villages.

Sheep farming also sculpted the landscape with stonewalls criss-crossing the bare shoulders of the landscape alongside the twinkling rivers and silent copses. Now the sheep have largely disappeared, but their legacy has provided Britain with one of its outstanding areas of both natural and built beauty.

However, if the outside of a building is a house, it is the inside that makes it a home and, fortunately, the Cotswolds has a visionary in Pippa Paton, whose vision and skill as an interior designer complements the work of Jurassic seas all those millennia ago.

These mellow buildings have provided the canvas for her to create outstanding homes through reworking both the spatial planning and interior design for modern living. Using the natural elements of the Cotswolds, Pippa transforms these interiors with natural fabrics, textures and neutral palettes to complement and accentuate the glory of the buildings themselves.

I hope that 'Twenty First Century Cotswolds', with its wonderfully diverse and eclectic approach to transforming the character of Cotswold houses and barns, will encourage and inspire. I feel sure it will.

View from Coaley Peak, Cotswold Way

RORY BREMNER

Writer, Satirist, Impressionist and long-time resident of the
Cotswolds and Scottish Borders.

Whenever I hear the words "traditional values in a modern context" I instinctively think of Tony Blair and New Labour, and a Steve Bell cartoon showing a copy of the party's totemic Clause IV sticking out of a waste paper bin.

Yet the adaptation of the traditional for a modern lifestyle is a constant challenge for any designer, and lies at the heart of Pippa Paton's unique style.

For what could be more traditional than the Cotswolds - that quintessentially English landscape, stretching broadly from Oxford west to the Severn Vale and from Stratford upon Avon to Bath, and characterised by its rural charm: towns and villages hewn from the distinctive limestone buried deep beneath the rolling hills that give the area its name - *cot's wold*, literally, 'sheep's enclosure in rolling hillsides'.

Here, Pippa has made her home, or rather, homes: from her own projects, transforming first a sixteenth century listed manor house, and later two barns, into exciting, contemporary living spaces while respecting and restoring the original stone walls and vaulted ceilings that gave the buildings their traditional character, to a wide range of other homes and properties across this unique area.

Restoring and transforming period houses is a difficult trick to pull off. Overdo it and the juxtaposition of traditional and modern jars; keep things exactly as they were and the house owns you, rather than the other way round.

With her love of traditional materials - stone, timber and slate, dramatically transformed using light and glass - Pippa brings an exciting, modern twist to traditional buildings, adding bold objects and statement pieces - a large clock, a Highland Cow's head in bronze resin - and not afraid to use cool, refreshing greys and blues or textured wallpaper to give effect to walls. Abandon taupe, all ye who enter here.

And yet, above all, these are houses that are fun to live in: functional, elegant, stylish, but also homely. Somewhere you love to relax and entertain friends - oh, yes, she cooks as well - did I mention that?

But that's another story. And another book.

INTRODUCTION

by

PIPPA PATON

People always say that you are lucky to do a job that you love. So, I must be doubly lucky. Not only do I spend my life working in interior design, I get to work with some of the most beautiful buildings in the Cotswolds. I am absolutely passionate about what I do; for me creating spaces and designing interiors, especially in character buildings, is one of life's great joys. I find it truly exciting when I walk into a space for the first time and see what it could become, both spatially and in terms of fabrics, colours and textures. Working with the client and my team to realise that vision is hugely rewarding.

Much of that reward comes from knowing that at the end of a project we will have created a home that people love living in. Creating a completely functional home which reflects both the style and lifestyle of its inhabitants is at the heart of successful design. The other great reward comes from knowing the work we do helps these properties evolve and remain relevant. When it comes to the listed and historic buildings of the Cotswolds, our designs and our clients' commitment is giving these buildings their next lease of life and helping to preserve their natural beauty for generations to come.

For decades, Cotswold interior design was quite traditional in style; antique furniture, heavy curtains and country kitchens abounded. But even though Cotswold buildings share so many materials and design features, they are surprisingly diverse in style. So, as we settle into the 21st century, it is really inspiring to see the breadth of contemporary styles that people are welcoming into their homes. From a Scandinavian pared-back approach and rustic and agricultural aesthetic through to industrial chic, luxe detailing and boutique hotel ambiance, all of these styles sit comfortably inside the stone and timbers that, in some cases, date back five centuries or more.

Whilst there is a growing diversity of styles, there is an underlying demand for functionality, ease of living, increasingly high-end technology and extremely luxurious amenities. This demand includes everything from underfloor heating and home automation to spa-like bathrooms as well as the addition of entirely new types of desirable space. Secondary and outdoor kitchens, home cinemas, wine-tasting rooms, gyms and yoga rooms are no longer unusual. Adapting these buildings to accommodate such demands whilst also complying with conservation guidelines requires careful thought and great consideration for the building and its materials.

Of course, the way of living has changed dramatically over the centuries. For example, we have moved away from the days of 'behind the green baize door' servant culture, where a series of small rooms catered for everything from flower arranging to boot polishing, to the 21st century desire for open-plan, multi-functional family homes. Not only has the way of living changed but many of these wonderful buildings were never built as homes but as hay barns, coaching sheds, stables and outbuildings. Whatever their change in circumstance, today we focus on exposing and enhancing their original features to allow the intrinsic beauty of the buildings to shine through, stripping back the faux and eliminating the pastiche to ensure the historic materials, craftsmanship and style is celebrated.

Whilst these buildings have withstood the tests of time, previous alterations and extensions and even for some the introduction of various modern amenities such as internal bathrooms, electricity and running water, few have survived unscathed and none remain, if indeed they ever were, straight and true. Therein often lies the root of both their inherent challenge and charm. These days, we are far more enlightened about the fabric of these buildings, their importance, and the need to protect them for the future. Which is why our approach to (re)designing them has become less invasive and much more focused on exposing, enhancing, and protecting their historic features and materials.

The large volume of some properties, such as barns, can also present challenges when thinking about the optimal use of space and how to make it both practical and comfortable. Creating distinct areas within the entirety of a space with different yet interconnected uses is a common desire. Small spaces, such as cloakrooms, often overlooked as being less important than other areas, can create surprisingly fabulous spaces with amazing visual impacts. The most important factor though is that the finished house reflects the integrity of the building and the functional needs of its occupants.

Another consideration is that the fabric of which these Cotswolds properties are made requires specialist understanding and repair, which is why I work with local Cotswolds specialists, craftspeople, and artisans. Many of these professionals work within a family business undertaking a trade that has been passed down from generation to generation. I find both their understanding of the area's heritage and their skills invaluable when it comes to transforming these historic buildings into homes fit for 21st century life.

Lighting and its control is another fundamental aspect to the enjoyment of contemporary spaces. This is particularly true when it comes to multi-functional areas such as kitchen/dining/living areas, where task lighting is required for food preparation one minute and an ambient glow for dining the next.

I am incredibly fortunate to have a unique and very personal insight into Cotswold properties in the 21st century. The examples featured in this book reveal both the amazing diversity of these buildings as well as the numerous ways in which people choose to live in them. The main theme of this book however is the passion to preserve the area's history, architecture and buildings whilst making them relevant to 21st century living.

I hope you enjoy this book as much as I have enjoyed creating the homes that are featured in it!

Old Sodbury, Cotswolds

RUSTIC
PERFECTION

A beautiful barn has been lovingly restored to
showcase exquisite original features with an
agricultural and industrial aesthetic

Sitting on the edge of one of the Cotswolds' most picturesque villages, this 19th century stone barn enjoys stunning views over the Windrush valley and is now a relaxing retreat for a family of six.

Converted to a dwelling several years earlier, the barn had initially been given many of the traditional features and fittings of a standard residential home. Tiled floors, a pine staircase and Victorian-style skirting boards concealed original stone walls, blue bricks and timbers which had the potential to bring the barn's exceptional spaces to life.

This renovation provided a wonderful opportunity to remove the domestic fittings and uncover the original fabric of the building whilst also introducing elements that have some sense of authenticity to the 19th century barn. The original barn doors now sit contentedly over the restored blue brick floor of the impressive double-height reception hall. A bespoke steel staircase and balustrade have been fashioned as if by a local blacksmith and work in complete harmony with the exposed stone walls and timbers.

The interior of the barn is set over three levels. The ground floor comprises a sitting room, family room, kitchen and a dining area all accessed from the main hall. The first floor houses two guest bedrooms and enjoys another double-height room in the form of the master suite with an ensuite bathroom in a 'floating box' above, affording enchanting views across the valley. Three further bedrooms nestle happily in the eaves of the attic.

The family has collected various items such as clay pots, agricultural tools and rusty horseshoes, many from excavations around the site, which are now fittingly displayed around the house. Select pieces have been imaginatively repurposed including an old threshing table now housed in a sleek glass coffee table, a set of vintage skittles that now form the main hall's rustic chandelier and an old stable door reincarnated as a shower screen.

The integrity of the barn has been restored and enhanced and the building now delivers all of the 21st century comforts and conveniences to the family and their frequent guests.

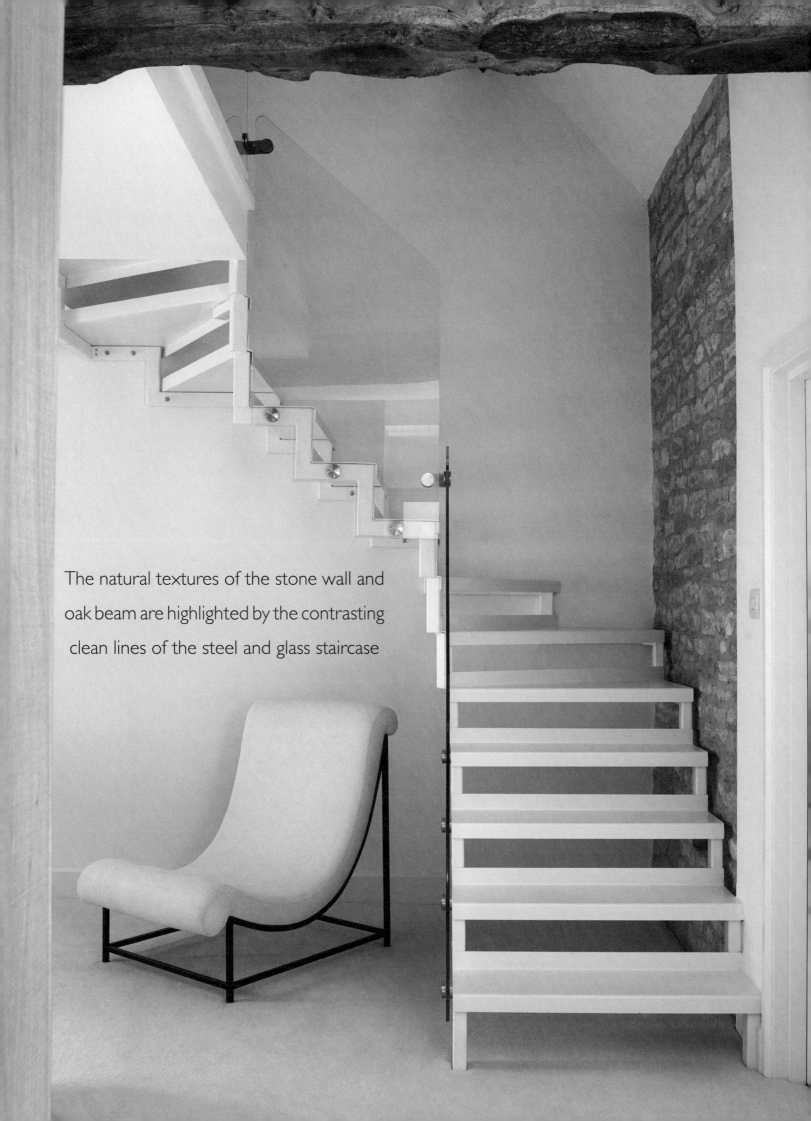

The natural textures of the stone wall and oak beam are highlighted by the contrasting clean lines of the steel and glass staircase

A contemporary steel staircase leads from the master bedroom to a 'floating box' above, which accommodates the master ensuite. The illusion that the box floats is created by the use of glass walls and a seamless white resin floor. This emphasises the original elements of the space such as the Cotswold stone wall and the arresting oak truss and purlins. Stunning bathroom fittings were carefully selected in keeping with the building's agricultural heritage and are displayed like pieces of art in a gallery.

The bespoke bath filler was inspired
by the river valley which the
bathroom overlooks

A split-level teenager's bedroom in the attic has built-in joinery doubling as
a headboard and innovative storage to allow the bed to face the view

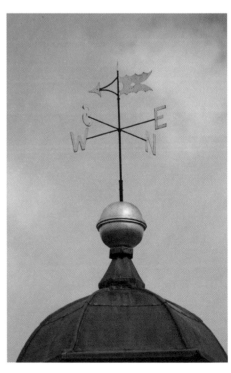

BLACKSMITH

SMITH WHINNEY

Having grown up in Italy, Jos Whinney has always loved the beautiful and ornate ways in which steel and iron feature in Italian architecture. Having eschewed the family business, he moved to the UK at 28 and took an apprenticeship with a renowned artisan blacksmith. It was during this time that Jos realised the unadulterated joy of being able to mould, turn and twist metal to his will.

Now working from his own workshop on the edge of the Cotswolds, his portfolio ranges from beds and staircases to bridges and gazebos. When I feel that metal is the right choice, Jos has become someone I work closely with to realise my ideas.

On occasion, I've come across a client's possession with sentimental value or a beautiful story and therefore real potential for a bespoke piece. In one case, I noticed a set of exquisite vintage skittles, bought as a special birthday present and with a lovely history of their own. Collaborating with Jos and a lighting specialist, we designed a steel cradle to encase the skittles and high-intensity LEDs in a stunning feature chandelier.

The resulting beauty of this unique piece is not found solely in the craftsmanship itself but in the long shadows the skittles throw on the hall's double-height walls. A precious, personal item is now enjoyed on a completely new level each time the couple set foot in their home.

The element of steel, whether shaped into simple or more intricate and detailed pieces, provides a remarkable complement to the natural materials prevalent in the historic buildings of the Cotswolds.

A SENSE OF
SPACE

A stripped-back Cotswold stone house

offers spacious, open-plan living

This late 20th century Cotswold stone house has been owned by the family for over 20 years. After a period of living abroad in a large contemporary apartment, the couple returned with their teenage daughters and decided a fresh approach was needed to living in the house. Whilst the property was the right size and in the right location, the flow of the layout and the use of space were now far from the light and airy open-plan living space the family were seeking.

A large-scale renovation completely transformed the internal space on both floors, signalling the beginning of this property's spacious renaissance. A large kitchen, dining area and vaulted sitting area have been created, each a distinct space but collectively creating an impressive effect. Features have been made of a glazed arch linking the outer gable wall to the main living space and a helical steel and glass staircase leading up to the first floor's glazed walkway connecting the daughters' individual suites.

Throughout the house, interesting finishes have been meticulously selected, such as the patinated brass door fronts on the double kitchen islands, a carved slate inlaid panel on one island and a curved glass base running through the length of the dining table.

Quirky touches were added; silver birch branches reside at the end of one daughter's bed and a trampoline is set in the floor at the end of the bed of the other. Floor-to-ceiling sliding dormers have replaced the original sloping attic eaves which has dramatically increased the usable space upstairs.

The ultimate deception of this home is that from the front exterior it appears to be an everyday example of a modern Cotswold stone house whilst inside it is a simple, minimalist, loft-style home for the family to enjoy for many years to come.

Patinated brass fronted units, plaited leather
and steel stools and smoked glass pendants
add texture to the kitchen

The master bedroom was opened up to provide a remarkable vaulted space with a glazed mezzanine level used as a study and reading area

Each daughter has a sitting room, bedroom and ensuite accessed from a glazed walkway across the main living area

FURNITURE MAKER

HUGO LAMDIN

Working from an old dairy that is now his Oxfordshire workshop where traditional tools and equipment sit alongside modern, cutting-edge machinery, Hugo Lamdin specialises in creating beautiful and individual pieces of wooden furniture designed specifically for a particular use or space within Cotswold homes. Focusing on longevity, Hugo takes great care considering the impact of the piece on the environment as well as its ultimate functionality.

Hugo celebrates, rather than disguises, the inherent flaws and characteristic textures of wood and cleverly combines the classic and timeless with contemporary living. Although wood is the dominant material, he incorporates other materials into his designs such as leather, glass and metal, using skilled specialists where necessary.

I have collaborated with Hugo on many occasions to create truly unique pieces such as a spectacular master bed made from a single tree that travelled only a handful of miles on its journey from tree to bed.

We have also designed a solid blackened oak dining table, marrying beauty with strength. With an elegant glass strip running through its centre hinting at the curved glass legs below, this highly contemporary piece of furniture gives the effect of being suspended in the air whilst simultaneously echoing the curved glass wall of the adjacent steel staircase.

This traditional material plays a key role in these exceptional interiors and Hugo's work provides real testament to the value of local artisans.

The hamlet of Petty France near Hawkesbury Upton, Cotswolds

ON THE
RIVER

A beautifully restored historic Dunkirk Little Ship has

been transformed for family days and nights on the river

Built in 1934 as a motor cruiser, *Lady Gay* is one of the flotilla of revered Dunkirk Little Ships which rescued allied soldiers from the beaches of Dunkirk in the perilous mission of 1940. Originally owned by Lord Dunhill, *Lady Gay* is now in the possession of an Australian family.

Lovingly restored to her former glory, the boat now spends her days meandering peacefully up and down the Thames, popping in to local regattas and making commemorative visits to Dunkirk. In 2012, *Lady Gay* took a leading role in Her Majesty The Queen's Diamond Jubilee Pageant.

The boat's restoration presented a set of unique challenges. The need to bring comfort, style and practicality into a small space was carefully balanced with the obligation to select finishes and materials able to withstand damp conditions. At the heart of the project was the desire to enhance the beautiful craftsmanship of the original design. The modern, functional interior emphasises the original polished mahogany finish whilst a timeless black and off-white colour scheme was introduced to add style and warmth.

The project has ensured that *Lady Gay* is now a hugely enjoyable and fun river cruiser for the family whilst at the same time preserving her exceptional history for future generations.

A NEW LEASE
OF LIFE

A restored barn provides the perfect backdrop for family life

and stunning guest accommodation

A converted 19th century barn set in five acres of beautiful, landscaped grounds has become the constant source of much-needed respite from the hectic lifestyle of the family.

Converted into a dwelling several years ago, it is only in its recent revival as a home for entertaining that the barn has really come to life. The large central space in the house has become its main focal point with an impressive oak staircase. Double-height oak entrance doors lead directly into a striking vaulted living space. Several distinct areas have been created using the structural elements of the space and thoughtful positioning of furniture. The formal seating area, complete with an opulent antique-mirror clad bar, leads to an intimate dining area beyond and a less formal seating area positioned at the opposite end.

Wherever possible, the original features of the barn have been restored and accentuated to acknowledge the building's origins. High-specification technology has been installed throughout the property to enable the couple to work from home and the family to enjoy modern family living.

The grounds have been designed to provide a formal courtyard at the front of the property around which sit the main barn, the guest barn and a soon-to-be developed gym and relaxation space which will complete the traditional farm courtyard. A large terraced area on the south-facing elevation of the main barn offers spectacular paddock views and space for dining under an arbour, an outdoor kitchen and bar, and relaxed seating area. The gardens boast a tennis court and cricket net for hours of real family fun.

The internal and external space of the barn has been revolutionised into a wonderful home perfect for entertaining large groups of family and friends whatever the weather brings.

The formal seating area, with an opulent antique-mirror clad bar, leads to an intimate dining area beyond

A petrified wood stool and faux fur throw add real texture
and warmth in the sitting area

An oversized stone basin and vintage comb mirror above the
bespoke vanity create a 'boudoir' effect

Beautiful original trusses are perfectly highlighted against white ceilings

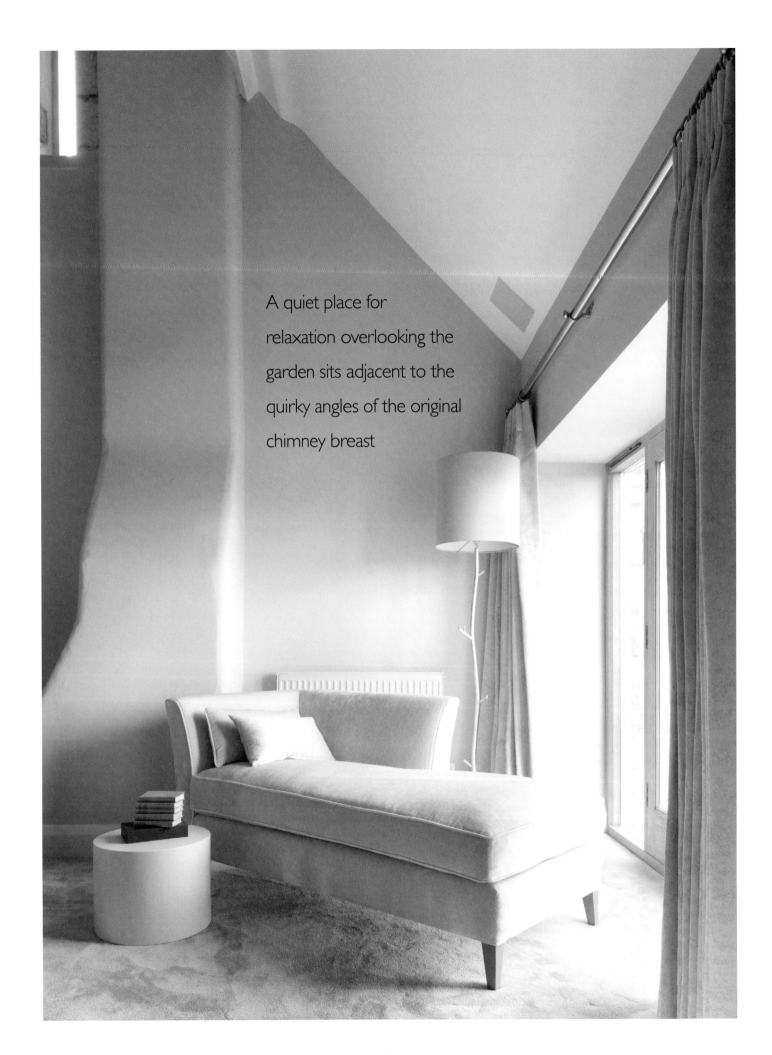

A quiet place for
relaxation overlooking the
garden sits adjacent to the
quirky angles of the original
chimney breast

An ancillary barn has been converted into impressive guest accommodation with an open-plan living space, four bedrooms and two bathrooms

A bespoke limed table and matching benches
form the focal-point of the guest barn

SOPHISTICATED
COUNTRY

A Grade II listed Cotswold stone manor house with a

contemporary pool and entertainment complex is now

a remarkable country haven

This historic, Grade II listed estate, set in extensive grounds, comprises a six-bedroom manor house, four-bedroom cottage, games barn, new-build gym and pool complex. When the family bought the estate, a three-year renovation project ensued taking the buildings back to their bare bones and completely landscaping the grounds, transforming the estate into a relaxing country escape.

Rather than opting for one large family space within the main house the family wanted to create several different areas where they could relax. The renovated space now includes a drawing room, study, family sitting room and home cinema.

An array of original features uncovered during the renovation were repaired and enhanced. Previously-neglected fireplaces in the drawing room and study provided elegant and natural focal points and the original hallway flagstones were refinished before being relaid over the underfloor heating.

Even though the first floor contained generously proportioned rooms, ensuites were carefully added to every bedroom whilst ensuring the space wasn't compromised. In the attic, originally used as the servants' quarters, two children's bedrooms, a bathroom and sitting room were created.

The estate underwent significant modernisation and, within the restrictions of a listed property, is as eco-friendly as possible at the explicit request of the family. A large biomass boiler, which burns wood pellets, was installed underground to heat the entirety of the estate. A full home automation system was installed to control heating and lighting including an 'all off' switch that allows all the lights on the estate to be turned off.

The beautiful grounds were landscaped, curved hedges planted and dry stone walling built to create discreet areas including terraces for dining and relaxed seating, an orchard, tiered gardens leading through to paddocks beyond, a private garden for the cottage and tennis court and cricket net area. The new-build gym and pool area enjoy their own gardens, terrace and pergola tucked behind new stone walls that provide privacy and warmth.

Stunning original flagstones were cleaned and calibrated before being relaid over underfloor heating

Instead of an island, a square dining table provides plenty of space for the family to gather and can be extended to accommodate larger groups

Glassware and pottery excavated from around the site during the renovation are displayed simply on a built-in kitchen dresser

The family are avid wine collectors so the old underground wood and coal stores have been repurposed as a cellar

The steps were rebuilt using the original flagstones and the vaulted brick arch was exposed, restored and highlighted with subtle uplighters

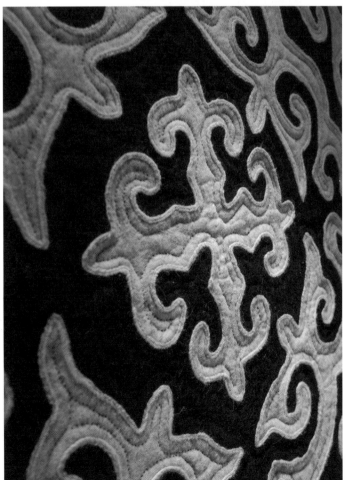

The master bedroom is accessed from an inner lobby which also leads to an ensuite and a dressing room which can be closed off with pocket doors

The bathroom's focal point is the view of a magnificent ancient
cedar tree which towers over the house

A new-build structure with a sedum roof houses a kitchen, sitting area, shower room and a fully-equipped gym which overlooks the pool. A picturesque vine-covered area provides welcome shade for relaxing out of the sun

MASTER STONEMASONS

OG STONEMASONRY

The Cotswolds is inescapably defined by its rolling hills and recognisable stone buildings and walls. The stone, formed from the oolitic limestone that lies quietly beneath the picturesque landscape, has been quarried for centuries. Not only is this stone beautiful, with its wondrous variety of creamy to honey-coloured hues, it is endlessly flexible. Almost every part of a building can be constructed from Cotswold stone. Its simple natural form is used for walls; whereas dressed stone is ideal for quoins, floors, cills and surrounds; and split stone is selected for roof tiles.

The stone's appearance in so many different forms is partly down to the extreme talent and skill of the stonemasons whose lives are spent taming and shaping the material. Like so many artisan crafts, the skills, and so often the physical tools, have been passed down from mason to mason over the centuries. Modern technology may allow for a better electric saw but the hand tools used for fine detailing have remained the same for hundreds of years.

Working across the Cotswolds, OG Stonemasonry undertake all types of projects from the repair and restoration of cottages and manor houses through to the iconic colleges and spires of Oxford.

The importance of the stonemason in building renovation and interior architecture cannot be overstated. In my own experience, it is often the more delicate aspects of the stonemason's craft that leave a lasting impression. The success of an overall project is often down to the smallest details and where a high-level of skill is required but often not seen, such as that required to repair and reinvigorate flagstone floors, breathe life into disenchanted fireplaces or to invisibly repair crumbling stone window frames.

In years to come when fashions have inevitably changed, the artistry of the stonemason will continue to maintain the beauty of these glorious stone buildings.

Arlington Row, Bibury

COTSWOLD

HIDEAWAY

A forgotten hay barn and three coaching sheds have been converted into a

light and welcoming hideaway in a soothing natural palette

A row of derelict Grade II listed buildings consisting of a hay barn and three adjoining coaching sheds have been renovated to provide exceptional separate guest accommodation within the grounds of the main farmhouse.

Substantial structural alterations within the original hay barn marked the initial formation of a new and inviting type of space. An open-plan living and dining area was created with an adjacent kitchen and the roof was raised to create the main bedroom. The original openings of the buildings were clad with soft grey vertical boarding allowing the exterior to retain the appearance of the original agricultural row.

Internally, delightful original features such as a stone fireplace lintel and a stone wall were uncovered. The foundation of the neutral palette was expanded with soft tones of grey and blue and simple furnishings were added so as not to detract from the building's fascinating original structure.

The wonderful outcome of this compact project is a tranquil, comfortable space for guests, whether they stay for a weekend or the whole of summer.

Snowdrop woods, Cotswolds

ECLECTIC
SPIRIT

Two Grade II listed barns have been seamlessly joined

with a contemporary extension to create a striking,

open-plan family home

Originally built in 1867, the barns had the potential to be a remarkable home and there was a clear vision for differentiating the old from the new. The two stone barns were joined end-to-end with a contemporary structure constructed of floor-to-ceiling glass and an anthracite steel panel roof. The new structure allowed the full length of the space and its various living areas to be seen immediately upon stepping over the building's threshold.

To achieve this visual effect, internal walls on the ground floor were removed along with all the doors excepting that to the back kitchen which doubles as a boot room. A low-level wall was constructed to separate the entrance hall from the sunken sitting room which leads out through sliding doors to the garden and scenic paddocks beyond.

The central area of the main barn with its original double-height openings softened by tumbling white linen curtains serves as a dining area to fully enjoy the space. A glazed gallery above overlooks the dining area which is adjoined by a cosy sitting area to one side and an industrial-style kitchen to the other. A convenient back kitchen is strategically placed to keep the debris of an ongoing dinner party hidden from sight.

Many of the barn's original stone walls in the double-height spaces have been left exposed and lime-washed with the oak trusses finished with a lime wax. To emphasise the contrast between new and old, the dramatic stone entrances to each of the original barns within the new structure have been kept in their natural state.

With the exception of the dark grey painted wood floor in the dining area, a pale grey resin floor has been used throughout the property. The walls are uniformly white to enhance the original features of the barn and to provide a canvas for eclectic pieces of art and sculpture, such as the bronze Highland cow by Tessa Campbell Fraser.

Lighting and its control are crucial when creating multi-use spaces in open-plan interiors and when highlighting key features. A variety of forms has been used in this house; simple downlights for task lighting exist amidst feature wall lights made from vintage Provençal roof tiles and stunning Murano glass chandeliers which draw the eye to the repurposed steel workshop bench functioning as a dining table beneath.

The barns now offer a stylish and functional home for all seasons. The doors are flung open in the summer allowing the external terraces to become an extension of the interior space, whilst a contemporary wood burner settled in the corner of the sitting room draws the family in during the winter months.

The bold industrial-style kitchen area in an anthracite finish features a stainless steel and marble island with a range cooker at one end, an acid-etched copper splashback behind the sink and a large salvaged French café sign

An alcove with wallpaper featuring cavemen-like drawings, an inset stone window and lamps fashioned from a vintage balustrade provides a quiet reading nook

A muted grey palette and textured fabrics allow the lighting and glass ornaments to shine in this restful room

Resin floors and textured wallpaper in the bathrooms create the backdrop for eye-catching pieces such as a revived stone trough and a hexagonal mirror

Simple, elegant fittings in the master bedroom, dressing room and ensuite bathroom are offset by antique finds: a Murano glass chandelier, a pair of vintage chairs and a carved wooden trough

SCULPTOR

TESSA CAMPBELL FRASER

essa Campbell Fraser is an acclaimed sculptor who focuses on life-size bronze sculptures of wildlife. Working from her studio in the Cotswolds, she has sculpted everything from guinea fowl to hippos. Tessa's pieces are displayed all over the world. Her work can be found in both public and private collections including that of Sir Jackie Stewart and Her Majesty The Queen for whom Tessa has sculpted her corgis and also *Estimate*, one of Her Majesty's favourite racehorses.

Tessa's work is incredibly detailed and finely realistic. Having personally taken one of her sculpture courses, I have witnessed first-hand the expertise and craftsmanship that go into every aspect of the process; from the initial sketches and the maquette to the life-size piece and ultimately the mould and the final bronze casting. What became clear to me over the course was that the beauty and strength achieved in the final pieces was the result of Tessa's deep knowledge of anatomy, innate feel for the material of her medium and a thorough understanding of the engineering of the final construction.

Tessa's pieces add a flawless sense of style to the interiors and gardens of properties across the world. I had always coveted one of her sculptures and designed the glass balustrade that overlooks the dining area of my converted barn specifically to support the Highland cow's head which Tessa sculpted.

Minchinhampton, Cotswolds

KIDS'
HEAVEN

A large attic space has been remodelled into a kids' heaven complete with indoor playground and innovative

reading, drawing and sleeping areas as well as a slide connecting them to the floor below

Seldom is there such a fun, concise and actionable brief for an interior design project. A family of five moved into a large single-storey Cotswold house at the beginning of summer. The attic conversion was to allow the three young children a vibrant, interactive area with distinct spaces for them to enjoy.

Attics always prove challenging with their pitched roofs and often non-symmetrical angles. The resourceful use of bespoke joinery created partitions between separate sleeping spaces for each child with leather upholstered reading holes and hidden storage spaces for clothes and toys. A designated 'fun zone' was created with a climbing frame, table football and playhouse set on purple rubber matting. In contrast, a 'quiet zone' for reading and creative play was constructed under a large window with a delightful view of the nearby lake.

Although the walls were painted white, colour abounds throughout the space in the furniture, artwork and floors as well as playing a crucial role in defining each of the bedrooms. This colour spills out on to the lower floor, evidence of the world above, as a new staircase with multi-coloured painted risers connects the two floors. The addition of a slide enables the children to get to breakfast a little bit quicker.

Every child's dream has been realised in this distinctly exciting and fun yet functional space. And 'slide tag' is now the favourite game of the attic's little inhabitants!

From drawing on the wall to sliding down to breakfast – this attic is truly kids' heaven

LIGHTING DESIGN

The days of lighting design being 'one pendant or two?' are long gone. The myriad of fantastic new fittings and luminaires, the increasingly complex technology and accompanying regulations coupled with the desire for flexible living spaces mean lighting design is now truly fundamental to successful interiors.

I often work closely with Jon Cardall from lighting designers Lightmaster-Direct who echoes this, saying "Lighting design for today's homes has never been so significant, with current trends moving towards multi-functional, open-plan living requiring lighting solutions which are as adaptable as the space itself."

Too often lighting design is not prioritised either through the failure to consider it early enough in the project or through budgetary constraints. My advice is to always design the lighting early on and to spend on its infrastructure before the actual light fittings themselves or even other items such as soft furnishings. Light fittings and curtains can always be purchased at a later date whereas lighting cannot be wired in after a certain point of the project. When renovating character properties, with all their idiosyncrasies and associated challenges, this is even more important as not all contemporary lighting solutions will fit or indeed create an effect in keeping with the building's heritage.

Creating layers of light within a space is unmistakably important; ambient, task, accent, effect and decorative lighting can all be ingeniously combined to support how a space is to be used. However, lighting design is far more complex than just the layering of light. There are numerous technical considerations behind achieving the desired result. The use of lighting control and whether it should be integrated with other forms of automation is as critical a decision as that of the styles and positions of the light fittings and their associated components.

Above all, consideration of the desired effects and ambience and the means of achieving it needs to be at the beginning and not the end of the project.

PARED-BACK
STYLE

A series of serene open spaces

decorated in a simple, understated style

have been created within a Cotswold

stone cottage

Built in the early 21st century, this four-bedroom stone cottage was bought by an American couple living in London who wanted their two young children to enjoy the fresh air and open spaces of the countryside at the weekends. The family desired a true country retreat which suited their lifestyle focused on art, music, cooking and the outdoors.

Challengingly, the layout of the house was that of a traditional cottage with small rooms leading off a moderately-sized central hall. Subtle spatial replanning opened up these rooms and simplified the circulation areas. Doors were removed and openings enlarged to enable rooms to effortlessly connect with each another. The master bedroom was expanded by moving the entrance, allowing space for a small dressing room and an ensuite bathroom. The wall between the children's bedrooms was replaced with joinery to afford two equally-sized rooms. Space was optimised throughout the cottage, reducing the depth of walls where possible and using every nook and cranny for a particular purpose.

The kitchen, designed to meet the family's specific culinary needs, was crafted by master cabinet makers from bleached oak-panelled timber, Cumbrian stone worktops, natural limestone floors and a repurposed vintage butcher's block. The small utility room was expanded into a utility/boot room with appropriate storage for the family's outdoor wear.

The restrained and uncomplicated style of the cottage has been achieved using a host of natural materials and muted tonal hues spanning greenish-greys to pale shades of stone. The carefully controlled colour scheme subtly pulls in both the colours of the surrounding countryside and the distinctive Cotswold stone of the structure. With the exception of the kitchen, pale oak flooring has been laid throughout the ground floor. The majority of the furniture selected for the house is antique, much of it being Scandinavian or French, whilst a wide range of natural fabrics including linen, wool and leather has been used throughout to soften the interior's aesthetics.

The owners are committed art collectors and new pieces chosen specifically for precise locations really bring the house to life. They are currently enjoying adding new finds to their ongoing collection.

A terrace with a barbeque area and a separate summerhouse with a veranda sit in beautiful gardens which truly finish this country getaway so that it can be enjoyed all year round.

Bleached-oak panelling continues from the kitchen into the utility/boot room which provides essential storage for outdoor wear

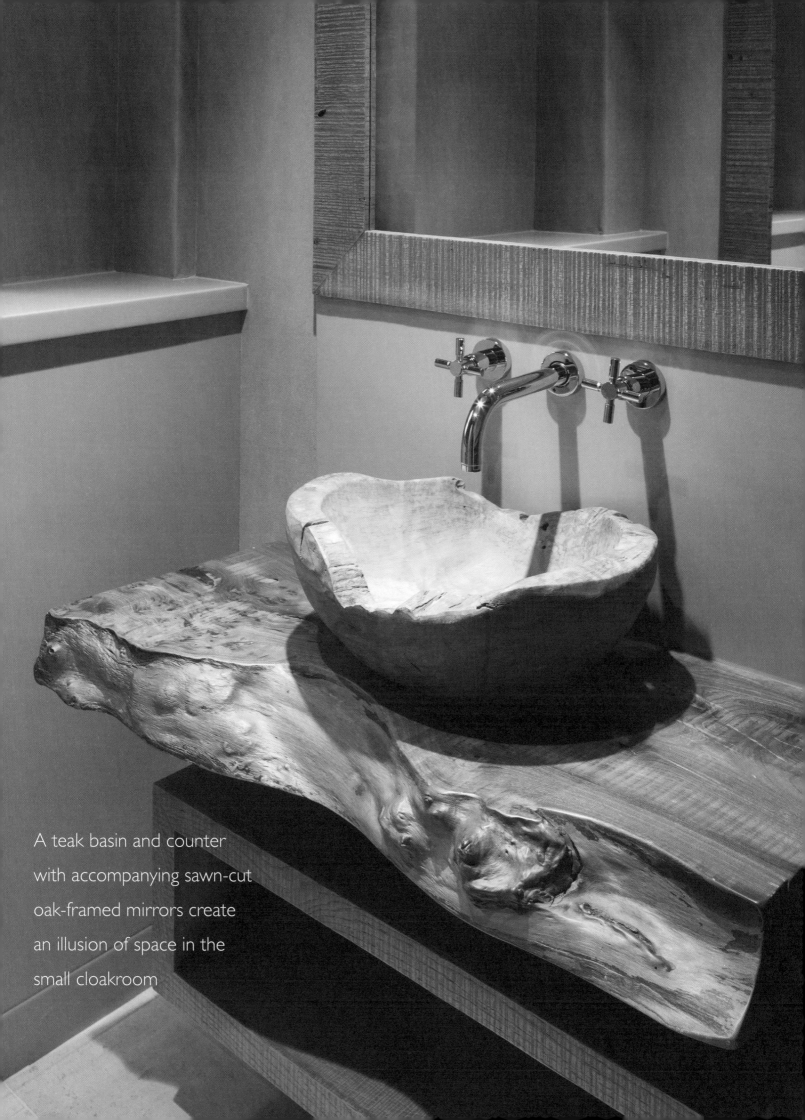

A teak basin and counter
with accompanying sawn-cut
oak-framed mirrors create
an illusion of space in the
small cloakroom

A simple French style in muted grey colours gives the master
bedroom an air of timeless tranquillity

POTTER
CHARLOTTE STORRS

Working from a peaceful garden studio in rural Oxfordshire, Charlotte Storrs came back to an early childhood love of pottery. Inspired by the simplicity of her Dutch heritage, she creates refined and minimal, yet highly functional, white pottery. Charlotte's recognisable style beautifully demonstrates that an economy of detail provides the key to forming pieces that work effortlessly in modern life whilst simultaneously complementing the natural textures of the Cotswold buildings I use her work in.

Charlotte's functional pots, plates and bowls are made from a rustic clay with a simple white glaze excellent for daily use. Charlotte's work is constantly evolving; she has recently incorporated Akebia vine from Japan into her work as this strong flexible material makes perfect handles. This beautiful, natural material just serves to enhance her simple and elegant pieces.

I have always had a deep love for pottery and it adorns my home in a variety of ways. From a set of bells I found in Portugal and white bowls shaped like the islands of my husband's native New Zealand to invaluable large pots and platters which we use every day, pottery has always provided a sense of timelessness and connection with the earth in both my life and work.

I have always been drawn to clean and fuss-free pieces whereas much pottery tends to be complicated and elaborate. When I discovered Charlotte and her beautifully simple, white pottery, I knew I had found someone who shared my sensibilities regarding this wondrous natural material. The clean lines of her pottery provide a lovely finishing touch when designing a 21st century room.

A SENSE OF
HISTORY

A contemporary family space fuses the interior of this 16th century

Grade II listed manor house with its gardens

All old Cotswold houses have a history and this manor house is no exception. Built in 1550, the house was then lived in by Sir William Ashcombe during the early 17th century. Notably in 1643, his widow Katherine entertained King Charles I on his march from Gloucester to Newbury during the battles of the English Civil War. The house was doubled in size around the year 1650 and a further extension was added in the late 19th century. The accompanying photograph from around this time affords a fascinating insight into the inhabitants of the house and their lives..

In the early 20th century the house was lived in by a wealthy landowner, Richard Staples-Brown, and his wife Makereti (Maggie) Papakura, whom he met whilst touring New Zealand. Maggie, a Maori guide, was renowned for guiding the Duke and Duchess of York around Rotorua's thermal pools in 1901. She brought with her to England an extensive collection of carvings, greenstone ornaments and feather cloaks which were used to furnish rooms around the manor house. The house was subsequently owned by the Butler family, who changed the name of the house to their own, and so it remains to this day.

When this Oxfordshire manor house was bought in 2006 it had been inhabited by the previous family since 1949 and had subsequently changed very little during that particular chapter of its history. Open fires were the only source of heat and the electrics were antiquated. The original servants' kitchen, pantry, flower room, housekeeper's office and a variety of coal and log stores were still in place, evidence of a long-gone era when the house was run by a team of servants. This warren of obsolete spaces from the past was astutely recast in the shape of the 21st century. A new eighteen-hundred square-foot extension houses a kitchen, dining and living space and large sliding glass doors connect the house to its seven-acre park-like gardens.

Original features discovered during the renovation have been left uncovered to embrace the history of the past. An old well in the boot room is lit from beneath and covered with structural glass and a medieval doorframe has been repurposed as a mirror surround behind a floor-standing stone basin in the cloakroom. Original doors and ironmongery have been refurbished, quoin stones brought back to life and an external wall has been exposed and celebrated within the modern extension. The roof was retiled using traditional methods and the original tiles where possible.

Lighting plays a critical role in the overall design of this home with task lighting, ambient lighting and decorative pieces such as the large copper lanterns suspended over the dining table all playing a role at various times of the day and when different moods are required.

The house has now been brought into the 21st century with all the amenities of modern-day life whilst retaining much of its beautiful history.

An old well has been exposed in the boot room and a medieval doorframe has been repurposed as a mirror surround

Rather than trying to make it light and airy, the lack of light in a north-facing room is embraced using dark grey textured wallpaper and atmospheric vintage lighting

A curved wall and balustrade soften the harder
architectural angles of the glazed atrium

COTSWOLD STONE ROOFING
HERITAGE ROOFING

The houses of the Cotswolds are a truly special part of our built environment brimming with many distinguishing features making them easily identifiable. Though few of these features are more beautiful and require more artisan attention than their stone roofs. Heritage Roofing, a specialist in stone roofing, expertly handle the alteration, extension and renovation of roofs connected with many of my projects. The skills of Shane Baldwin and his sons, third and fourth generation stone roofers respectively, are highly sought after across the region. Their work on heritage and listed buildings include ecclesiastical, National Trust and English Heritage properties.

As with so many facets of all great local building styles, Cotswold stone roofs are a product of the local environment and real ingenuity. Hundreds of years ago when it became evident that the local oolitic limestone could either be split by hand or naturally split by frost, creating flat plate-like 'tiles', it didn't take long for a successful system to develop to use them as a convenient roofing material.

These tiles are hung in diminishing courses with the longest to the bottom (Cussoms and Followers) and the shortest to the top (Short-Cocks). In the days when there were no gutters, diminishing courses developed from the need to throw water well clear of the walls of the building which was helped by using the large slates at the bottom. Now typically secured by nails rather than the traditional oak pegs, the tiles provide a totally natural, strong, long-lasting and beautiful roof that symbolises the character of the Cotswolds, which is so often the envy of the world.

Planning the courses, preparing the stone and actually hanging the roof takes years of practice, and these skills are often handed down through the generations. The notable extent of stone roofs across the Cotswolds, allied to strong conservation guidelines, has kept all the associated skills alive both in quarrying the stone and hanging the roofs. The workmanship Heritage Roofing brings to these projects helps to ensure that the famous stone roofs of the Cotswolds will remain the distinctive feature they are for centuries to come.

FASHIONED
ORGANIC

Two cottages have been remodelled to provide a

modern sanctuary from busy life and an ideal space

for entertaining

 London-based couple took the decision to relocate to the Cotswolds to a home which their two grown-up daughters and four young grandchildren could visit at the weekends and during holidays.

The house and its gardens required complete renovation to provide the spaces both inside and out for the couple to entertain and spend quality time with their family. Over the years, the property had been extended to four times the size of its original footprint and it needed comprehensive redesigning. Key to the redesign was a kitchen with space for informal family entertaining and separate formal and casual spaces for relaxation. Narrow corridors were widened by removing unnecessary cupboards, old flagstones were relaid, services were upgraded and bathrooms were repositioned to return bedrooms to their original proportions.

The house was decorated in a modern country style with a light palette of colours and using an assembly of natural materials such as wood, stone and leather as well as beautiful textured fabrics. In some instances, an entire room's décor was built around one of the couple's beloved pieces of art whilst the theme of travel was more generally reflected throughout the property in a collection of wonderful, unique items.

A new, refreshing relationship was forged between the house and its surrounding landscape to allow for easy outdoor living and an enjoyable environment for the grandchildren. As well as a practical terrace for entertaining and a private one off the master bedroom for idyllic, unhurried breakfasts, the grounds now encompass a pool with an unassuming shed-style pool house, a tennis court and a wild flower meadow. However, the pièce de résistance is the award-winning raised vegetable garden which is the owners' pride and joy.

The end result is a house and gardens with marvellous family-friendly spaces where time with the grandchildren can be truly enjoyed.

The irregular walls and uneven alcoves of the original kitchen weren't conducive to the modern country style that was desired. A streamlined finish was achieved through a wall of bespoke units, stepped forwards off the existing wall with panelling at either end giving the impression of a piece of furniture

Unusual finds add interest in the arresting cloakroom,

a space often forgotten in large projects

PHOTOGRAPHERS' CREDITS

Copyright © remains the property of each photographer as credited below:

Sven Arnstein Page 9 (top)

Joseph Baldwin Page 230 (top row right, bottom row right)

Tessa Campbell Fraser Page 164 (top row left & centre, middle row left & centre, bottom row)

Agnes Clark Pages 204 (top row right, second row, third row, bottom row), 205

Association of Dunkirk Little Ships Page 61

Clients' Own Pages 50 (left), 237 (bottom right)

Graham Coleman Pages 12/13

Country Life Picture Library Page 7 (top)

Paul Craig Pages 1, 5, 32-51, 54 (top row right, bottom row right), 68-95, 108-111, 118/119, 121, 124, 125, 255, 256

Sally-Anne Guibert Page 9 (bottom)

Elena Harris Page 55

Hugo Lamdin Page 54 (top row left, middle row left & middle)

Lisa Lloyd Photography Pages 128 (top row, middle row, bottom row right), 129

Vanessa Naylor Pages 164 (top row right), 165

Pippa Paton Pages 52, 53, 59, 60, 62-65, 69 (bottom right), 128 (bottom row centre), 132, 230 (middle row left)

Scott Paton Pages 66, 67, 178 (middle row centre)

Michael Paul Pages 206/207, 210-217, 218 (top left), 220, 221, 223, 226, 228, 229

Charles Richards Page 164 (bottom row left)

Steve Russell Pages 102-107, 112-117, 120, 122, 123, 124, 128 (bottom row left), 133-139, 178 (top row left & centre, middle row left & right, bottom row left & centre), 179, 218 (bottom row left & right), 219, 222, 224, 225, 227, 230 (top row left, middle row centre & right, bottom row left) 231, 238-253

Rachael Smith Cover, pages 14-29, 30 (bottom row left and middle), 54 (bottom row left) 194, 195

Charlotte Storrs Page 204 (top row left & centre)

Tamara Tovey Pages 10, 185, 202, 203

Nick Turner Pages 2/3, 4, 6, 7 (bottom), 8, 56/57, 130/131, 166/167

Jos Whinney Pages 30 (top row, middle row, bottom row right), 31

Matthew P Wright Pages 11, 96-101, 126, 127, 140-163, 164 (middle row right), 168-177, 178 (top row right, bottom row right), 180-184, 186-193, 196-201, 232-236, 237 (bottom left), back cover

ARTISTS & SCULPTORS' CREDITS

Charlie Barton Page 251

Tessa Campbell Fraser Pages 142/143 (Highland Cow), 145

Rory Cornegie (courtesy of Sarah Wiseman Gallery, Oxford) Page 78

Melanie Deegan Page 195

Michael B Edwards Page 45

Lucas Ferreira (courtesy of Sarah Wiseman Gallery, Oxford) Page 18

Laura Hart (Surface House) Pages 154,155

Frederico Infante Pages 192/193, 194

Sue Jones (courtesy of The Brian Sinfield Gallery, Burford) Page 79

Simon Ledson Pages 102/103, 105, 157

Stewart Mackay Pages 136/137, 152,153

John Maxwell Steel (courtesy of The Brian Sinfield Gallery, Burford) Pages 72, 80 (right)

Brendon Mogg (courtesy of The Brian Sinfield Gallery, Burford) Page 83

Katrina Pechal Pages 1, 71, 92

Jason Philips Page 223

Michael Ponder Page 156

Steve Russell Page 224

Bianca Smith Pages 118/119, 121

Hazel Soan Pages 138, 212/213

Tom Stogden Pages 126, 127 (bottom row left)

Peter White (courtesy of The Brian Sinfield Gallery, Burford) Pages 17, 80 (left), 81

PUBLISHING DETAILS

First published in the UK in 2017 by Pippa Paton Design Ltd. Text, photography, design and layout copyright ©2017 Pippa Paton Design Ltd.
All rights reserved. No part of this book may be reproduced, stored in a retrieval system or transmitted in any form or by any means, electronic, electrostatic, magnetic tape, mechanical, photocopying, recording or otherwise, without prior permission in writing from the publisher.

Publisher: Pippa Paton Design Ltd. and Momentum Books

Copyright © Pippa Paton Design Ltd. 2017

Art Direction: www.hughes-design.co.uk

ISBN: 978-1-911475-14-9

Printed and bound in the UK by Think Digital Books Ltd.

ACKNOWLEDGEMENTS

I would like to thank all of my clients featured in this book for the opportunity to showcase their wonderful properties. It is always such a privilege to be allowed an insight into a family's world when working with them on their home.

Thank you Mark Hedges for your beautifully written foreword and Rory Bremner for your fabulous preface.

I would also like to thank all the people who have worked with me to bring my ideas to life, the artisans, tradespeople and specialist contractors, whose commitment to excellence and attention to detail is absolutely instrumental - I couldn't have done it without you.

Thank you Laura for your commitment, dedication and creativity.

And thank you Rob and Tim for your unending dedication and for always listening and working with me on even the most challenging of projects.

I would also like to acknowledge and thank Hughes Design for their tireless efforts to turn my original design of the images and copy into what you see here and to all the photographers and artists whose work features in this book.

Most of all, thank you to Scott, my husband and business partner, for helping to bring my visions to life, without whom none of this would be possible.

PIPPA PATON is a multi award-winning, industry-recognised interior designer and spatial planner who is the Founder and Design Director of Pippa Paton Design Limited, an interior design, architecture and project management studio based in Oxfordshire. The studio focuses primarily on historic and character Cotswolds homes, transforming them for 21st century life. As the studio has grown the vision has remained clear: to create stunning spaces that bring together contemporary and eclectic furnishings whilst enhancing the architectural and heritage features of the inspirational properties they work with.

Whilst Pippa has always had a love of colour and texture and an instinctive ability to see the potential of a space, she studied business at Exeter and subsequently entered the world of finance. After qualifying as a Chartered Accountant, Pippa worked in advertising where she spent over a decade as finance and group commercial director of some of the UK's largest advertising and media groups.

Inevitably though, the desire to express her own creativity won out and she set up the studio in 2006. Pippa's approach to design is less about a 'style' and more about elements of texture, light, neutral colour palettes and the fusion of furniture styles and eclectic objects of interest. Pippa is now internationally recognised having featured three times in the globally prestigious annual 'Andrew Martin International Interior Design Review', with projects shortlisted for the Society of British & International Design awards for the last two years and with articles in interiors publications across the world. Her comprehensive 'black book' of artisans, crafts people, suppliers and contractors is crucial in helping the studio deliver the excellence, precision, detail and creative solutions for which they are renowned and saw them feature in Country Life's 2017 'Secret Address Book' of the top 100 interior designers, architects, landscape designers and builders.

Pippa lives in Oxfordshire with her husband, Scott, their two children Max and Scarlett, dog Summer, three cats and two ponies.